In the Buddha Factory

IN THE Buddha Factory

Alan Soldofsky

Truman State University Press
Kirksville, Missouri

Copyright © 2013 Truman State University Press, Kirksville, Missouri, 63501
All rights reserved
tsup.truman.edu

Cover art: photo by Suon Touhig. Used by permission.

Cover design: Teresa Wheeler

Library of Congress Cataloging-in-Publication Data

Soldofsky, Alan.
[Poems. Selections]
In the Buddha Factory / Alan Soldofsky.
    pages cm
Poems.
ISBN 978-1-61248-088-6 (paperback : alk. paper) — ISBN 978-1-61248-089-3 (ebook)
I. Title.
PS3619.O4324I58 2013
811'.6—dc23

2013023569

for Pamela, Adam, and Neal

Contents

Part III: Hyperreal

Acknowledgments

The author gratefully acknowledges the following publications in which poems from *In the Buddha Factory* first appeared, sometimes in a slightly different form.

DMQ Review: "Palm Haven," "Present"
The Georgia Review: "Melville"
The Gettysburg Review: "Anniversaries of Autumn," "Beyond Where I Have Ever Traveled," "Wandering Around"
Grand Street: "The Beginning of Summer"
The Greensboro Review: "Millennium Jukebox"
The North American Review: "Awakening"
Poetry East West: "At West Lake," "Morning Postcard"
Poetry Flash: "Sense of Place," "Twirl"
Rattle: "Early December" (originally published as "Early Night"), "Recovery at Lake Tahoe"
The Rattling Wall: "Country"
The Rumpus: "Of Its Occasion"

My grateful appreciation to the many friends and colleagues who have read various parts and drafts of this book, some multiple times, and who have been a sounding board for my work over many years; especially to Tony Barnstone, Darrell Dela Cruz, Stuart Dischell, Kathleen Lynch, Samuel Maio, Sandra McPherson, David Mura, Daniel Tobin, and to Joyce Jenkins and Richard Silberg of *Poetry Flash*. You renew my faith in the possibilities of poetry. Thanks to a research grant from San Jose State University and the California State University, and a Literary Arts Fellowship from Arts Council Silicon Valley, I had the time and resources necessary to complete this book. Also my abiding thanks to Jim Barnes, poetry editor, and Nancy Rediger and Barbara Smith-Mandell, editors at Truman State University Press, for their professional guidance and support in the preparation of this book, and for their work on their New Odyssey Poetry Series. And special thanks to my sons, Adam Soldofsky and Neal Soldofsky, for taking time to give their unvarnished opinions. And to Pamela Pennington for reading my poems at all hours, and for her unswerving love and support.

Beyond Where I Have Ever Traveled
—for Pamela

You've gone ahead
into the paralyzed sunlight, past the rinds of pastel
apartment houses, worn down
in the wake of morning's overcast
to the color of sand.

The residents—
in ill-fitting swimsuits and robes—
summer renters like us with only slightly more dignity
than dogs, scratch their flanks
roasted red by yesterday's sun.

There are so many of them
housed so close together, still they seem stunned
to see across their stainless steel coffee mugs another
face tilted slightly away, eyes stained
with the same imprint of sky.

No wonder you wanted
to get away early, before the newspaper racks
announce what is actually befalling this strip
of boulevard that cowers like an addict
in a damp sleeping bag beside the ocean.

To stop and ask where anyone
is coming from is forbidden at this time
of the morning before the 737s exit
the catacombs of air to disgorge their human contents
onto this pseudo-tropical shore.

That is why,
I wish to God I could keep up with you, love,
as you stride the three miles down the boardwalk
that fronts the beach, like the Pacific's own discarded foreskin,
to a table at the not-yet-too-crowded sidewalk latte shop.

And then walk back,
crusted with the salt of health,
the wind's idiotic intelligence blighting my countenance,
while on a skateboard a shrunken, platinum-haired man in baggy shorts
and Jesus T-shirt passes by me, saving the rest of the world.

I: Present

Present

Here, in the blue sheen of the present
vanishing even as it arrives, I want to
give you something, a present
although it is worth less than the string
of pearls I can't afford to buy.
It is only this arrangement of words,
with which I hope you will adorn yourself,
my description of you. Beauty so practiced,
a rendition of Helen's colors chosen
to allure. The first time I saw you
I couldn't help but keep the contours of
your countenance in my mind, the way a
live oak keeps its leaves. It cannot exist
without its canopy. You prefer the sleek
hardware of a tropical breeze that makes
each part of you tremble. Let my gift be
that well designed, to be indispensable
as the sky. Something you would keep, that may
not seem important but that will
in the rondure of the night while you sleep
remind you that love is here, even if
it needs from time to time to be repaired.
That it's ubiquitous as water
spraying from the nozzle
when you shower that continually runs
down the drain only to be replenished.

Sense of Place

Ten a.m.: towers along Market Street
mirror the sky, the street still in shadow,
almost in another climate.
I'm swept up in the crowd
that pours into the Palace Hotel, where in 1930

Warren G. Harding died—some conjecture
from poisoning. After Teddy Roosevelt
spent the night in Yosemite on Glacier Point
he said, "Bully." John Muir and the Hearst newspapers
made it famous.

A place is more real when you imagine it.
In Yosemite Valley there are three hotels.
In the meadows beneath the monoliths
buses run every five minutes. Hordes walk amid the oak
and cedar. I attempt not to notice.

————

I'm one thing in one place, something else
in another. When I drank champagne
on the deck in Belvedere gazing at the houses
on the hill above the harbor,
I felt oppressed by the beauty.

The skyline across the water
too bright despite the overcast,
my eyes numb with the bone-white glare
of summer. Drake dropped anchor
a few miles from here.

He wrote of a month of "stinking fogs"
and named the headlands he scavenged New Albion.
Some claim he missed the bay altogether,
that he marked his damp, bitter days farther north
lost in some colorless recess of time.

––––––––––

It's important to learn the birds' names.
"A man who doesn't live in nature
as a stone does or an animal,
will never in his life
write two worthwhile lines."

In the central Sierra, there are Steller's jays,
western tanagers, red-breasted sapsuckers,
solitary vireos, chipping sparrows.
I can't identify them without a guidebook
in my pocket.

Birds learn their songs where they are born.
The fledgling duplicates its parents' call
in the deep nostalgia of the branches.
When he was caught in the brambles,
my then two-and-a-half-year-old son Adam

pointed to the blackberry thorns
and excitedly repeated his new word: *prickles.*
It became a joke between us.
When he didn't want to go to bed
he'd repeat it so I should remember

running terrified through the neighborhood
calling him. I found him one street over

scrunched down behind a house overgrown
with trumpet vine and jasmine.
Roosters and mourning doves call

through the dawn beneath the roar
of jet planes. This place was once called
Rancho de San Antonio, deeded by the King of Spain
to Luis Peralta. What we call hills are not *hills*.
They are mountains.

Palm Haven

Wind breathes behind the curtains as shadows
distill in noon's fermented light.
Look, as the air warms, how insects swarm
out of the grass, brilliant specks
that swim about our faces in a gritty cloud
whose undulations make us bat our eyes
as leaves fall, melting away
into a frail debris that encrusts the yards.
Here we are exiles among angels,
in this district of exquisite surfaces
where crowns of Mexican fan palms float
above the street on their slender poles.

What sort of God would consume us,
soft-bellied and salt-stained, who stand
in the knots of shade eyes pointed at our shoes?
Or who stroll sandstone paths, past
earth-colored columns hung with lanterns,
each dangling over an urn planted with ferns and flowers.
A murmur of bees in the honeysuckle,
a fountain making its sleepy music.
The heat clots in the folds of our sleeves
as a jet passes over, the drone
shaking the hinges of the trees,
and seems to fill every pore with reverberations

that scrape us to the very bone
before it subsides.
In these spacious hours
the product of our labors is stillness.

The sprinklers click on with a sound
resembling someone rapidly snapping his fingers.
The imprint of my steps,
evaporates on the pavement
while I sit out on the patio staring
into the vacancies of afternoon,
sun marking my skin with
indecipherable initials and signs.

Early December

What lies the sun tells
        a few leaves stripped of color,
parenthesis of rust on the hinges of the car door.

A cricket singing
        beneath the clump
of verbena beside the porch.

High cirrus
        lit by something
that has fallen.

The edge of a storm front
        coming, a change in the smell
of the air, a quiver in the wind.

The house quiet except for
        the gnawing in the attic.
The sound of a sound

that barely holds the weight
        of being heard, a remnant
that ripples down the hallway

into the room where
        you slept. Your books still
dozing on the shelves waiting for you.

The darkness, smooth as licorice.
        The only light in the house
the one in the closet left on since morning.

The Beginning of Summer

A brightness in the skies even after dark,
a remnant sun splotch. Backlit turquoise
deepening to indigo, then black.
Lavender afterglow of clouds over Mission Peak.
The wind's delicate sharpness on my neck,
as if dusk were a saturation of lyricism.
Intolerable beauty, heartbreaking by definition,
and we are relieved by its passing.
After the 235 steps to the bottom of the cavern
our guide turned off the lights. Total darkness.

"Put your hand in front of your face,
you *think* it's your hand you see."
I had a feeling almost giddy. The mind sees what it wants.
It's why lovers close their eyes when kissing.
I could not see a single thing,
words from my eyes did start. Difficult
for that to continue. Small interruptions—a child's anger,
breakfast dishes, getting toilet paper.
I am appalled by the sensation of being

governed by the body. Swallowing, yawning, having to pee.
The expected and incalculable distractions—
car pools, dental appointments, the boredom of children.
How easy to give in. To do nothing
and let the hero become the absence
of narration. It's easy the second week
of summer, heat washing the wide streets,
air yellowing over the valley, altocumulus
scattered and sullen, and, of all things, rain

like a crystalline dust spattering the concrete,
leaving a smoky, acrid scent of evaporation.

The child won't get dressed because
he wants to wear the stretchy black bike shorts
with pink fluorescent stripes
and black tank top he's worn the last three days
on the camping trip. But they're in the wash.
So, naked, he wanders about the house
wailfully because what I have laid out for him—
the seersucker shorts and light blue T-shirt
I thought he'd be cool in—isn't *cool*. What in nature
can be more hurt than him?

What if the least daylight could harm him?
His blood photosensitive, so that to live
he had to be kept where it's dark
like the two girls whose strange affliction
I remember from television. Who could only at night
be outside their house with the lead curtains,
rising to eat breakfast in the dusk,
then going out to play, the moon their sun,
their birds the owls that by day
sleep hidden in the sultry trees.

Give in. For a brief second in the cave,
I thought I glimpsed how we make the world up
with words. How we lie to perfect memory.
After it rained, gnats swarmed through the ruins of light,
the evening turned lustrous. Vireos flitting about
the chamise and bear brush, a few stars in the east.
A small wind stirring the oat grass, rustling
the digger pines up the slope and the sycamores below
along the creek where two boys crossed the shallows,
balancing from rock to rock in the twilight's slow perishing.

Attraction

At the restaurant the light pooled
in her hair. And about her shoulders
the scent of verbena lingered

as we sat across the table, posing there
savoring the other's look, covering
the other's silence. The wine at last urging us

past the perimeters of our strangeness,
letting flickers of conversation flare,
the glow of our words wreathing our faces

through dinner like an aromatic smoke.
Yes she said when I asked if she would
share dessert. By then even our spoons clicked.

I didn't want her to go after the waiter
cleared the coffee. And tried to think
of something I could say so interesting

or inexplicable it would keep her
from announcing it was late,
that she had an early appointment.

I shouldn't expect her to go home
with me. It was too soon, my poor tongue
too unreliable. I was in trouble.

So I asked if she would like to share a cigar
a writer I knew she'd heard of sent me
from Cuba. Yes she said if I walked her to her car

parked far across town. Which I did—
walking with her through the night that promised nothing
more than to hold us a while in its arms.

Anniversaries of Autumn

So much for the days I can't remember…
But should because I see them pending on
the calendar, the dates like lit windows

in a building across the avenue,
windows I hardly notice until in one of them
I recognize a face and start to panic.

I, who strive to be inhabited by words,
unable to put together the idea
with the thing itself. A sheaf of paper,

spilled open, pigeons pecking for crumbs on
the sidewalk or poised above on a wire
as though ready to descend, a deafening flutter

cascading down. An unctuous residue
on the pavement. It isn't difficult
to find this place on the map of your going.

Let's say it's by a river, let's say I'm
supposed to meet you at a particular time
though I can't, because I can't remember

what it was I had agreed to. Only
that there is this date circled, not in red—
the black numeral underlined in pencil.

Underneath a sketch someone's made of sun-
beams slanting through clouds. What am I missing?
What anniversary or augured occasion?

What saint is sitting at a bright table,
awaiting a rapturous arrival?
The water murmuring, lapping against

the pier, stock sound track beneath the gaps in
conversation. This absence regarded
as unforgivable. No matter how

inadvertent one's attention is drawn
elsewhere in the flash dazzle of the day.
You are drinking coffee—or chardonnay.

You might have said something to the waiter
before you took out your money and stood up.
What else could happen as he scrapes the tablecloth?

My voice on the cell phone intermittent
in the static, my pledge of apology
subject to atmospheric conditions.

The words themselves spaced, so that anything
could pass between a sentence and its meaning.
The scroll of weather, best an abject mood.

Love can fade without prompting. A baby
we're told bonds to its parents' faces. Thus, we gaze
at each other, fixing the other's gaze.

Possessing the face we want. The wind sweeping
up the seeds of desire as the leaves fall.
Until nothing is left, nothing floating

in the folds of air above the traffic.
Until we can hardly remember what we were
and when we stopped wanting what we wanted.

Fall

Do you know how hard it is to see you
walking around every day on this strip
of 14th Street, in the village
of perpetual beginnings, where the dry
cleaners spills its shaft of neon onto
the puddled concrete? You invent want.
Suddenly, I am reminded that people
are like pumpkins, that they rot from the inside
out. So, I'd better thank Victoria
Chang from whom that line was stolen, for
remembering Larry Levis, who broke
every decent piece of stemware in my house,
doing his Mick Jagger imitation
at 2:30 (for God's sake) in the morning,
the divorce after-party finally winding
down. I didn't want to move the contents
of the hutch anyway, and once it fell,
it was part of the fallen world, left to
mix with the ten thousand shards of rain
the air would carry. This is the time of year
the sun is paralyzed, clouds lowering the edges
of the sky. How can I live without you,
as the warmth slides out of the asphalt while
my grip grows looser and my skin too tight.

Melville

You cannot loiter long in this downtown library branch
without being asked what you're looking for. I said
I always wanted to read *The Lives of the Squids*.
The librarian mentioned that there were three volumes.
She looked me over like I was an olive
in a root beer glass. I'd rather do origami

than read about the construction
of innocence in the nineteenth century.
I'm not a formalist, but I can read inscriptions
on a crypt as well as the next guy. I'm tired of living
on salt pork and whale fat. Bored with looking
into the dead mouths of coelacanths.
She looked at me as if I had taken something
unspeakable out of my pocket.

She said she could look up *mollusks*
on her computer. *Cephalopods* I corrected.
That's when she explained that there was a prejudice
in this district, dependent as it was on the bovine economy.
Excuse me, I said. I said the truth was I had recently fractured
my knee, which caused me to speak on several topics
at once. What was I saying just now?

She looked so sweet then, so terribly thin.
I barely stifled an impulse I suddenly had to touch her ear.
I'm sorry, I said, but I had lost my thought. As she tilted
forward I could see her forehead's waxy gleam,
her pasty, white neck, the light slipping down
the modest slope of a breast. Oh, I was lost.

By the time I came to my senses I realized
I was standing inside a whirlpool. There was no way I could
go back to what I had been doing, parsing sentences.
Doing piecework. I had to shape up.
I had been drowning in pages of water.
Living in a group home. Surely I knew that the truth
slanted. What sad harpoon had I lashed myself to?

On what bone had I been gnawing?
I had consented to the doctrine of filth only
because what else could one do? How could I have
not seen the taxicabs idling, their signs turned off?
It was time to go by then. The air
was being shut off a little at a time.
There was a lance in my side. She was saying
something. She was telling me a fable
about obedience that I didn't already know.

Country

We're out in the *cuts*, my son says—
the *boondocks*, they used to call it. We're looking
for a way back to the tollway, but
we're getting nowhere. We're somewhere
near Aurora, Illinois, land of Wayne
and Garth, where kids come home to live
in the basement. In the backseat, my other son
asks how many ways are there to use *rat*
fuck in a sentence. Let me think, I say.
"To cut taxes again for the rich
is to *rat fuck* the entire country."
"To cut the pensions of retirees
is to *rat fuck* every employee in
the company." Despite my best efforts
to be cheerful, my face is a map
of worries. I get lost staring
in the mirror. Nothing looks the way
it does on TV. But what can you do?
I drive into the long twilight,
the dipper slowly unveiling itself
over us. The sky is no protection
from this anxious yearning to be elsewhere.
Along the road trees rear up that look like smoke,
gray pines with needles that appear no more
than a smudge of feathers. We look for a sign
to Naperville when we come to a bridge
over a greasy river covered with fingerprints
of the moon. A star streaks through
night's jelly. Another, then another.
I've always thought to get something you've got

to give something up. But
out here where the earth is flat enough
that you can see the argon glow
from the National Laboratory on the rim
of the horizon you get nothing.
You just get to give something up.

Figure

All summer stranded in some linguistic
Chula Vista, waiting for the other shoe
to drop—such a one-storied existence.
Here's a dissolute boulevard of strip malls
and parched figures of speech, where there's nowhere
to shop for images except at one
of Broadway's twenty-odd liquor stores,
or for discounted similes at WalMart.
She said she would be okay on her own
in the store, that she'd know what she wanted
when she found it. Besides, she added,
she could look for herself. That's fair enough.
The heat outside sufficient to drive even
the fiercest Mexican hairless indoors.
The air sweet as patchouli oil, congealing
under the tin-roofed promenade that passes
for a downtown around these parts. She said
she'd keep her cell phone on, figuring out
outfits to try. Her figure less svelte than
she'd prefer, though her face no less surely
diaphanous. This to distract herself
from the pestilence, black flies hovering
over the health and beauty aisle, fat as
bullfinches, clinging to the window screens
at home. The house almost under water
according to the figures, no life jackets
stashed up in the proverbial attic.
The fog coming in like an accordion,
its sallow breath wheezing in queasy chords.
This could go on for a while. She is not ready

at closing time, still in the dressing room
changing her combination of garments,
looking better than what's aglow over
the horizon, that smudge whose unctuous,
raw, acidic tincture troubles the sky.

Extract

We wait while they read the ribbon
of your blood, to see if you're well enough
to take the medicine that undoes you,
that corrodes the constellations of your cells

that don't grow as they're meant to. On
even numbered days you say *no*, feeling
the barometer of your body drop too far.
Then we go back to the car, parked

on the street where the name of every store begins
with *Y*. When you get okayed to get hooked up
you request a turkey sandwich
from the Fearless Deli, whose onion breath

wafts into the moldy December sky. It's then
I think everything about the way we live
is wrong. Maybe if we eat half the meat
our skin won't dim so fast and slacken,

so why not extol each smoky eyelet
of water that dampens the sidewalk as we make
our way up Fillmore to the Tapas bar.
When they told me what they'd have to extract

to preserve you I was at dinner. When I left
I forgot my cell phone, but the waiter came
running out. We adore the considerate.
I know a kiss isn't enough to relieve

what afflicts you. Still every day I came back
with a video to watch on your computer, to rearrange
the garden you've tended in your room. On
the day you go home you want a hot dog or

a chicken salad sandwich. Something good
and ordinary, something they can't give you.
They tell us to build you up, they tell us
you need fish oil, turmeric, an elixir

of açaí berry, a certain mushroom extract,
to pack saline in the gaps of your incisions,
to keep friends' visits short, that you need
each day to walk a little further, to get a bit

of sun, to eat frequent small bland meals, to keep
your electrolytes up, to try acupuncture,
guided relaxation, anything blissful. That it would
be enough to prepare for the way ahead.

Record

It's almost too much to bear
witness on foggy mornings before nine o'clock,
to the driveway across the way,
jackhammered and bulldozed up
into a dump truck, our whole house vibrating,
debris strewn in the engulfing dust.

This is what it feels like when the phone rings,
an electronic mist beside the bed,
the mumbling, not remembering
something important that might have been said.
What explanation is there for how
we've endured all this?

The failures of improvement, as if aging
should improve us. But you are better,
the house a record of what's kept intact
your imagination. White lacquer drawer fronts
flush in an island of red granite
variegated as a coleus.

A white bowl above eye level on a red shelf,
like a clay balloon. The kitchen an oxymoron
of filled space. When you left the hospital
we needed boxes to carry what friends had given you,
vases like tubas, bouquets and orchids.
Through the corridors a trail of petals.

Bad news doesn't get better with time.
It became necessary to keep a notebook,

to record the hour, to list the substances you'd ingested,
even hunger as it modulated. Some food
you once liked made you sick or didn't taste
right. We had to concoct a better diet.

It had to be the right color, more orange
more yellow. Yams and salmon, acorn squash;
no nuts, no whole grains—not yet. No sugar.
Nothing from a cow. Nothing corrupted by
industrial agriculture. I stopped
shopping at Safeway.

You could only rebuild yourself with clean
ingredients. And through the long months
of treatment, the chemicals dismantling
your body, its blue and lavender veins accentuated
by the cold you felt even on warm days.
Your cheek smelling of decayed jasmine.

It's June again and you are hungry
to plant red geraniums and a new plum tree,
to re-enter the garden under a thin trellis
of spring clouds. A tingling in your toes,
in your fingertips, you can't say from where.
It could be the end or the beginning.

The neighbors stand amid the detritus
directing the demolition of their porch
while a cement truck disgorges its heavy music
as if there was nothing we shouldn't miss
out on. Not even the dementia of construction
intruding upon this soon-to-be scar of memory.

What would be the point of preserving

ourselves if we couldn't tell
if what is in the air can be described
as perfume or smoke. Or if we didn't know
whether the body could recover, or if confusion's
sorry racket was for now to be everlasting.

Awakening

Awakened by mockingbirds
in the stale August early light,
sky the color of tallow,
she goes to the sink.

Sleep crusting her eyes, crumbs
of mascara under the blue slits, hair brittle—
not a person to become, she thinks.
No one she can recognize

glaring back from the dull sheen
of the mirror. With her fingertips
she smoothes the lattice of creases at her temple,
puckers her lips, making a face—half sneer

half kiss—as she rubs her cheeks
with the washrag she keeps out
for guests. No one to say anything
about this, about the extra weight

that's settled around her hips, her
sore feet. She puts her tongue
between her teeth, the roof of her mouth,
like sour honey. The taste of a story

she once read aloud of the girl
lost in a forest. Darkness descending.
No shelter. Who knew to say her name
backwards three times, to wrap her head

in her arms so she would be kept
from danger. Now she is the twelve-fingered one
who devours children, who'll someday be pushed
into the oven. A picture on the wall

over her shoulder. A portrait of snow,
she with her tribe of angels. How she's tried
to re-inhabit that radiance. The house
quiet now, as porous as skin.

A husk of perfume still lingering
in the bedroom. A remnant of sweetness
mingled with the brine of bedsheets.
And air smoldering in empty rooms.

II: In the Buddha Factory

In the Buddha Factory

Form without a body, body without form.
Where we start and where we end.
You remember ascending the hillside
through the green expanse of afternoon, mist

dripping off the ganglia of mulberry
a few pink blossoms already exploding,
quavering in the low wind.
In the temple, the abbot fished in his robes

for his cell phone, surprised at such
ringing in the world. In a cloud
at the top of the mountain
you found a staircase leading down

to a fat statue, leafed with golden moss,
mouth open, laughing. So difficult to
tell what is genuine. You saw hundreds
like that one arranged for display in the showroom,

rows of them in various postures, washed
in the commodious tinctures of commerce.
Bodhisattvas male and female, some with
red fingernails, waiting to be sold

to resorts in Las Vegas. Nearby the world's
largest Buddha is being assembled in a shed
like an airplane hanger. Its nose about
the size of a Learjet. You can't help but bow

and mutter prayers. It's good business
the manufacturer says, his own father
a believer. You couldn't know you were
here to prepare for the hard silence ahead

when someone close to you labors for breath,
flesh dimmed, an insolvent spirit, the nurse
feeding him morphine, an ampoule an hour,
one eye lolling open as if to see

beyond the light. Then there's you rubbing
a spot on the top of your head, looking
away at a normal face on TV,
to distract yourself from death's disheveled

taxonomy. Outside, in the jaggy water
of the marina, boats lull at anchor
repeating the sea's endless detachment
from the weight of its occupants.

At West Lake

A small breeze shakes the leaves
        beneath a tea-colored sky.
Boats bob on empty water.

A man lives only inside the face
        of the language.
Words are the air and the grass.

Evening looms in his eyes.
        It comes always later,
after the lines of the mountains have blurred.

And the smell of rain drifts
        across the strange pockmarked
bellies of rocks that outlast

poetry, which is what cannot
        be named, a breath
coming up off the soon-to-be-wet

sidewalks where no one is walking.

               West Lake
               Hangzhou, China

Zhejiang Postcards

Autumn Snow Temple

Obedient boats.
No snow in autumn,
only white flowers.

Taizhou in Spring

All morning mist carves
        the edges of mountains.
Air the color of steel.

Escorted, our bus rolls
        along wet streets,
faces wavering in the glass.

Half asleep my words
        disappear like peach blossoms
in the rain.

Trouble in Hengdian

A man climbs the hill,
weight of the full moon
on his shoulders.

Early Morning Postcard

Six a.m. I feel the gray lips of the wind
        on my skin.
Most of the old frogs that sang last night
        have jumped back in the pond.

A man knows that his words are like
        a candle factory, a flickering façade—
a row of windows glistening across the road
        through the mist.

The path uphill to the temple is slippery,
        smeared with streams of mud.
But can be negotiated.

When I get up I stoop over, my beard
        rough as old newspaper.
My tongue blank,

the past tense of the rain
        writing its musty taste inside my mouth.

Hengdian, China

New Century Hotel

i

Enough is not enough.
           Every night a banquet.
Sixteen dishes—the second is dessert.

Poetry makes the mind porous
           just as wine does
or dancing across a bridge
           over a river of crocodiles.

A man must write his poem
           in a fast hand in the dark
before daylight comes
           and condenses it.

ii

I am a scholar of afternoons
           not mornings

Mornings, you will find me
           in bed at home, half the world away, snoring.

June mist burning off
           while I turn over with a sigh.

Wenzhou, China

At Yandang Shan

For ten days I've been looking
        for my shadow.
Lost amid the outlines of mountains.

At last the sun is out,
        green halos shining on the spires
of the peaks.

It won't last. These words,
        too, are only souvenirs.
The wind has picked up.

Soon the rain will come again,
        drawing its beaded curtains
around the cliffs.

I long for things that are hard
        to imagine.
The color of water

falling out of the rocks
        into the white spaces
of departure.

Here I am gone even before I leave.
        My words holding on
without me to the cliffs.

Yandangshan, China

Arriving Back in California

Defined by sunlight, the waxy leaves of the camellias
       waver in the wind. I know how time moves
only in one direction. But today is an exception.
       Flying back across the dateline, I've arrived before I departed.

So I can relive the day that started with the pointillism of rain
       in Shanghai, the taxi stalling on the expressway.
I can remember the future, my shoulder jammed
       against the seatback and my legs folded

under the seat in front of me, a video of sleep
       running behind my eyelids. Clouds brushing
the wingtips. It comes to a still point,
       this always rushing forward. The lunge of landing,

filing into the jetway, entering a haze of fluorescence
       where everything turns white, my ears still stopped up.
Furiously chewing the air in my mouth. Something
       I kept so long to myself I've swallowed it.

But the day repeats itself. Is this what stuns us?
       Or is it being here, the bleached hills a magazine's idea
of paradise. Threads of poppies flashing in the grass,
       each adding itself to the vernacular of May.

The landscape so unbearably familiar. Shadows sharp
       under a China-blue sky. The hum of bees beneath the trellis
in the rising heat indifferent as the desolation
       stirred by a fan's slowly moving blades.

Wandering Around

In from the airport, heading back into the sprawl,
I'm scrunched down in the leatherette
backseat of my ex-wife's new Accord,
my head filled with soft cheese.

I'm ready for a pillow,
still testing the sadness, like a new word I haven't
learned to use, or a pair of shoes not broken in,
unyielding as the notion that we are raw
passing facts, pummeled by air,
shivering back on earth as we do
in thin summer clothes.

I don't want to be the man blowing the leaves
as the dry heat heaves into October.
I don't want to be head of the family,
to squint at numbers intractable
on stock reports or read silvery tables
of fine print buried in the business pages.

I don't want to plan for death like a person
remembering the future. I don't want to lie in bed
three brittle hours each day, fretting about
a bologna sandwich, and worrying
if I can get a banana before dinner.

I don't want endless finales on the telephone,
to bequeath a legacy so charily concocted
it can't be decoded, except by those
licensed to piece together pages misfiled
in the blue cabinet of the wind.

After landing, I waited a half hour for my baggage.
The carousel going 'round seemed interminable,
but in retrospect was momentary, brief as a splash of water.
I waited with my briefcase slung over my shoulder,
holding in its padded recesses all my memory.

How long ago was it I learned to drive the '55 Fiat,
orange carpet tiles on the ceiling to absorb the shaking?
Or hitched a camper to the back of the Galaxy,
caught in a thunderstorm, brilliant,
in the folds of the Boston Mountains?

Who knew that life would stretch a lifetime?
Or what my franchise would be
after I rolled the canoe in the White River, clawing
the rocky bottom, my father yelling
"put your head up," as the sky lurched at my panic?

Or on the all-night drive across the Mojave,
who woke me up to see the dipper
slide over the flayed outskirts of San Bernardino?
I don't want to be the man who pulls over
to drink tea from a thermos, checking the map
for the precise exit. I don't want to forget things
I imagined happened, before I'd seen
a freeway or uttered a complex sentence.

I don't want to be like the man
who scorned the first person, who made me
me. Who shaved off my facial fuzz
with my mother's Norelco. Afterwards
he'd sit at his desk with a snifter of brandy,
one ear plugged into Hayden or Mozart
playing through a transistor radio,
and grade papers.

He hit me once because I had called him Hitler.
He used to send me away to practice
the piano. Once he rifled through my drawers
finding Gauloises and Salems. How my room must
have stunk, but that's not what bothered him.
It was that he couldn't perfect my imperfections.

I don't want to be the man who converts
to buying gemstones. Who enjoys
numbers for their rational biographies.
My head is swimming. I see we're getting close
to home, where a light mist curls beneath the sodium
vapor lamps. I know I'll need help
to get the bags out of the trunk.

In almost sixty years on the planet
I've never been without him. I need to take
my vitamins, to start a low-fat diet.
I need to walk more, wander around the neighborhood.
According to him, few of our men have strong hearts.

Target

That man with the dented, hand-lettered sign
standing on the weedy island at the entrance
to the PW Market parking lot feels it.
On his head a filthy visor, scorched
a reddish orange, and the sun pressing down.
I see him when I go next door to Walgreens
and later on my way into Target,
my own face broiling in the glare,
my feet steaming inside the sauna of my shoes.
What embarrasses me isn't what he asks for
and that I don't give it
but the way he waits there, eyes drooping,
making us sealed in our cars responsible
for him. It's as though he's on exhibit—
the weeds and the chain link fence
around the vacant gas station, strewn
with pieces of the wind.
A few drivers roll their windows down
and thrust bills into his hand. Most
keep their eyes forward, occasionally glancing
into the melting sky, all of us hurrying
to get to the next place. It's maybe 100 degrees
and the streets gleam like sheet metal.
These are not the streets of martyrs
but Milpitas where a procession of shoppers
files in and out of automatic doors seeking
air conditioning. A jet glides overhead
heading toward San Francisco,
the city of cool, while I drive
into the blistered light loaded down

with things I have to have. He's sitting now,
leaning into the sliver of shade his body makes.
Stopped in traffic, I feel myself
reach into my pocket.

El Eden

We fly down here to get warm,
to this fingernail on the Costa Verde,
surf crashing in the mind's postcard.
Iguanas slithering down whitewashed walls.

Our hotel rises fourteen floors
out of the jungle, bougainvillea dripping
off balconies "with sumptuous views of the bay."
Sometimes, things look better in the literature.

Today the air smells of diesel infused with iodine,
a cloud of algae floating in on the tide.
Mist like a torn negligee flung over the serrated ridgeline.
Only a few Americans come here for the holidays.

A chorus of hammers ricochets
from the dry swimming pool.
Workers labor shirtless 'round the clock
to repair the luminous pit.

And we put up with it. Who wouldn't
trade the kiss of a Margarita
at sunset for a little inconvenience
after a day of braising the flesh.

So we drink to the health
of our country, bereft,
waving the flag until midnight
amidst the ruins. "Another round, *amigos*?"

We can endorse their politics.
"If the poor devil's at the end of his rope,
cut him loose." The mariachis' lament
swells with nostalgia for the condemned.

Ay…Yie, Yie-Yie.
We throw *pesos* at the sea
of black sombreros, applauding the stars'
costumed celebrity. Down the long stairs

the waves erase the beach's history
of footsteps, an unfinished conquest.
Here's where Ava Gardner met her lovers
on the set conquistadors from Hollywood

constructed, overgrown with hibiscus
and coconut palm, tendrils everywhere
invading the shells of adobe walls,
the doorways dissolved

as they are every place
from which we've been expelled.
We who are free to trek unendingly
through paradise, in rented Jeeps and Volkswagens,

chased by skinny, homicidal dogs,
trailed by jewelry vendors into muddy villages
where beer is cheaper than water,
and temptation more available than sunshine.

Friends Café

—Casperia, Sabina Hills

Swallows throng the piazza
        as the noon hour swells with a haze
of human speech, a cloud
        of diphthongs drifting past
toward the folds of blue hills
        and raked fields with their fringe
of cypress and olive trees—
        ordinary things overheard
I don't understand.
        Each bird diving down for
something invisible,
        its trajectory
unplottable as the moment
        unfolds its fraction
of a second here and gone.

Slight

He asked her to stroll with him in the garden,
the woman composed from his own rib,
who helped him discover sleep
is the remedy for loneliness. For a while
she listened to his excuses
about why they should do nothing
and eat only things labeled organic.
She said *hey check it out, man, it's all
good. You've got to try one of these apples,
red as a mirror. The snake said you'll see God
so much better.* But then he did not know
any snake, much less one who spoke. Even
though he could understand every animal
language. He thought for a minute,
listening to the beasts singing their work songs,
and birds saying their prayers. Anyway,
where do they go, outside this garden? They'd
have to be mad. *Snakebit* he said aloud, thinking
he'd been slighted. How unfair
she knew they were naked and he didn't.
And that the sun sets from left to right. Boy,
could she read him. *Okay* he said, and took
a bite. Right away he began to panic
about the future. He heard a voice in his head
say they couldn't stay now that they knew
what the gig was. And thus the sky turned white
over them as they looked back at the garden.
Who had they slighted, that His reputation
should be ruined, even when He was alone?
He couldn't even say the name—his own

and all his lineage cursed? What bullshit.
The garden left to snakes. They followed
a dry river, and learned that they could drink
sand. She came up with the idea of those fig leaves.
They could start a cottage industry. As
for children they could make miniature
replicas, anatomically correct,
and cover them. So what if there'd be slight
imperfections. How bad could it be?
Yes they'd have to work, but if there were more
of them, they could still achieve dominion.
And if the crops fail they could go further
east. Along the way they could make up stories
and whittle things out of the salt brush. Nothing
would ever happen in Mesopotamia.
He told her to try to make something that
could hold their stories, a container, something
where he could keep the sheets of skin into
which he'd scratched his slender marks. That later
he figured some anthropologist
would dig up and sell to men in black gowns
who'd believe absolutely everything.

Slide

Athwart the fizzle of a winter late
afternoon, I slide down into a sort
of basement. Another attempt to get
to the inside of things. Some kind of warehouse
or museum? A Roman catacomb
with a bar at the far end? The dark is
a sentence with a gap in it ... like a mirror,
something neither true nor false, or like a word
you can't actually pronounce—such as
synecdoche—that comes in handy when
criticizing the décor, your point drowned
out in the barrage of techno pumping
through the woofers. It doesn't matter
how much you try to cover your chagrin.
You still feel the heat rush into your face.
That's when the maître d' with a severe
Moroccan accent asks how many there
are in your party. That's when I can't even
count to two. Still he shows us to our booth—
the VIP section, all sleek white leather
and metal, the subdued color designed
to dazzle. It doesn't matter that I
can hardly hear what I'm saying. A leg
upholstered like a cloud presses against
my thigh. Oh, on the menu so many
brands of vodka I don't know what to choose.
The woodwork is posh, the ceiling startlingly
blue. Upstairs, people walk on metal plates to
cross the sidewalk, where they can get a look
at photographs projected in the lobby

of a Tony Bennett look-alike
overseeing the building's restoration.
This group has forgotten how to be solemn.
When asked for her ID a girl in black
hikes up her skirt. The security guard
lets her pass. Although he is dressed for war
he'd rather dance. Because of my connections
I'm in the inner circle. Believe me
if I were not already here, I would
have no faith that I could explain myself.

In the Air

Above the frozen western slope of what
I imagine to be the Defiance Plateau,
named by some sore-footed surveyor
after the fort that sat in the draw just across
the Arizona border—twice abandoned—
from which Kit Carson was said to have set
eight thousand Navajos out on their malnourished trek
southeastward to internment in the Bosque Redondo,
I see many wrinkles.
The courses of rivers diverted and broken
through a scattering of mountains
scored by a cuneiform of roads cut
into the grayish brown, scrubby undulations
of an earth so unpopulated that from here
settlements melt into the landscape,
which I notice only as small abrasions
of lights below the wing after dusk.

———————

Where do they go, the people that belonged here?
There seems little to stay for except for those
of an indigenous genome or who
pursue the delirium of uranium.
Radon seeping up under some of the houses,
like hatred rising to the surface.
It's then what I think of is *placement.*
Where do they place those who need to be moved?
And what can they do with those tailings
that get the little clicker of the Geiger counter chattering?

———————

Then there's my mother
who abrades anyone who comes near her.
Don't tell her *Tuesday* if she thinks it's Monday.
There can be no truth. Only she cannot live much longer
in the three-bedroom rancher

with knotty pine paneling and 1960s
bathrooms that she occupies alone
with a cat known as Velcro, and with
the assistance of an obliging, middle-aged Nigerian,
a leaky oil-head and yellow cake émigré
to whom she writes malignant checks.

———————

Where does the air go when it's sucked out
of a room? When it whooshes
through a grate beneath the window
in a dim rectangular chamber
where someone in a raised bed is hooked to meters
and tubes? I'm in a pressurized cabin,
six miles up, listening to Ry Cooder
through my iPod sing about an alien
who drag races the Mojave salt flats.
What can I do? Each day, the saying goes,
is just another, the sea still in its chains
soundless. And me, back on the ground
at home beside the ocean, beset by morning.

III: Hyperreal

Hyperreal: Virgil
in Los Angeles

—after Sandow Birk's *Inferno*

In the canvas, you blink dust
out of your eyes, gazing into a perpetually
burnt sky as if remembering

the future. You lead tours down
defaced and fiery streets. But your hunger
for misery seems unsatisfied.

In this translation, a sentence is half heard; a page
half deciphered. The key doesn't fit
the lock, the car won't start.

So your imago will not make it over
to the home for the last supper
with parents who dribble silence

onto their pastel velour sweat suits.
Your excuse: it's too warm in the dining room,
the food infused with high fructose corn syrup.

Though you're certainly one who knows the way
through this bizzaro city, where the boulevards
end at the beach beside the ash heaps.

From the heights you overlook the set
of the golden gate snapped in half in the distance,
clad in remnants of light, spanning what's not there.

You always get what you've postponed—Skid Row's
motto engraved atop the golden arches, "Abandon all
hope on entry here." You stand with lost souls

from downtown like Whiskey Dan
who each afternoon takes a cab back to
the house of pain. You can't expect him

to follow directions. You must drive him
to the brink of this flaming canyon
where the architecture must burn.

You know it's not wise to stop here, but you've come
to discover what future remains: *Chevron,*
Ikea, Carl's Junior, Sears, WalMart.

Perhaps some lesser brand will light the way
out of the shit storm. You've driven
half an hour to find a restroom.

Here's a gas station, but the privy's chained.
A figure silhouetted against the molten edge
of darkness hands you his card. Tells you

go down a few blocks. The experience repeats.
Even after there's nothing there's still
traffic; the ramp ahead

as far you as you can see
clogged with a blur of brake lights. A plume
of disconsolation hangs over the avenues,

occludes the trashed emblems of suburban
civilization. The marquees and mausoleums,
the shuttered Giant Burger with its charbroiled sign.

An oil derrick on the precipice still flexing
its sinews like a demonic bird pulling
from the exhausted earth a larvae of flame.

———————

"Whiskey River Take My Mind" is the tune
you want to hear, looking down at these freeways,
winding through the gashed and gnarled city.

From the arroyo cable cars ride up the side
of a smoldering hill, framed by date palms.
This could be Brueghel's version of L.A.

after the next quake, its downtown towers
looming against—if can you believe it?—a volcano spewing
along the horizon its sulfurous steam.

Or Hieronymus Bosch's San Francisco
burning again for its sins. It makes you want to lean
over the rail to better see the disaster coming

You hope you won't succumb to the pressure
to admire the grandeur. The apocalypse in 3-D.
Below, an inundated city awaits to incinerate you.

You can't rewrite the Book of Revelation
or concoct a new book of nightmares.
Nevertheless, it's your pleasure to gaze upon the ruins

to merely circulate among the spectators,
and watch crows land on the high-tension wires
while you shield your eyes against the view.

Sympathy for the Devil

—for Charles Simic

Only ants know the devil
still exists, despite what it says
about brooms in the ancient books.

See how they tunnel down
into the crust of the earth,
sorting hieroglyphs of dirt

which they carry back
to the surface where
they mill about or converse.

Would-be semaphores awaiting
orders from the invisible,
from the dark one

who has tricked us before
with sweetness, who steals
our friends, who says

our faith has failed us,
that we are imperfect.
Why is it that the prophets

so often declared us doomed,
confirmed relationships fail, and pleasure
ceases to satisfy after all the hours

spent in its pursuit? Look
how hard these creatures work
for their reward, to elude

annihilation's heel. While we pray
not to be crushed by the sun
to which we offer up our flesh.

How much do we know
about what goes on in the world
we feed on and that feeds on us,

or why it disgusts us, that tale
about the decomposition
of the soul? How difficult

to be without a body,
an intelligence that riddles
this grist of dust.

Only ravens would bask
in the afterglow
of our extinction. But they know

they'd have work to do,
to scan the windfall of the air
with their radar, searching

for something to pick at that once lived
like us, that could behold
in the bare sky the rim of heaven.

Of Its Occasion

—a revision in progress

Oh, what do you think? Fewer peacocks
in the pine woods. A tableau of moonrise
over wan foggy hills so picturesque
it would best befit a canvas. How to
illustrate the difference between what *is*
and what can be seen—as if description
is the thing that lingers, an aftertaste
of sight? A sweet chewiness, like raisins
for the imagination? The *raison*
d'être. An idea that outlasts at least
a summer's day? The hero acts for us,
our representative from Connecticut.
(I'd imagined this in tercets.) But then
he speaks, and we can't truly stand his voice.

Do you understand what I mean? I mean,
isn't that what the rain says? Or perhaps,
because it doesn't rain these summer months
it doesn't matter because we can imagine water
falling on the sidewalk, we've seen it. But
now the houses are made of sun, and the
hours mount steeply toward what blisters the eye.
Isn't it speech that makes the visible
a little hard to see? One cannot say
so directly. Nonetheless the wind chuckles
in the branches of the jacaranda,
and flies light on the pyracantha in
the actual heat. (I used to think *pyro-*
cantha—fire in a can. Not so wrong?)

We know that these are merely words; we know
their power to control the way the world
seems. Just call it artifice. What to do
if something serious happens, like a
glacier melting? What language do they speak
in Greenland? Much less what to do when the bank
breaks, this civilization would become
more relaxed, everyone in blue jeans
growing food in the backyard. Unspeakable
the names of the starving, the dead honored
for not living. Instead, we pretend these
transparencies of sound, a flowering
of sirens and orange cones on the thruway.
The signs that mark evacuation routes.

I suppose the mind's correspondence is
exquisite, the origin of the tongue.
Yet such commodious polyphony sucks
the dry warmth out of eucalyptus leaves
whose fragrance is a memory of dappled
shade, of a maze of backyard gullies,
fences melted into a reverberation
of curves. The underlying ground giving
way to dust. Why should anyone remember
this? The past as big as space, the blue that fell
from the abstract sky. Was it naked then,
some forged truth charting the weeds, the lemons
more yellow than a raft of adjectives?
In such phrases we found our daily bread.

Wordsworth in Santa Cruz

Before the flood he lived on Love Creek Road,
and with his sister read Tarot, flipping cards
on a red velvet scarf outside cafés
along the Pacific Garden Mall. From the point
he watched surfers in black neoprene paddling out
sleek as otters, lining up to catch the head-high sets
and get pounded in Steamer Lane where the waves break
both right and left, and in the backwash
the water sprays up through itself like smoke,
as if the bay were composed of cold blue flame
that smolders against the rocks. In the parking lot there'd be
the usual dross of VW vans and Rancheros,
people half undressed, toweling off, brushing sand
out of their suits. Overhead a flock of cormorants,
winged migrants, trolling for fish or garbage.
At dusk he'd head back to his cottage,
a garage behind the boardwalk, where the wind
had scrawled obscenities in the dirt in Spanish.
Swallows making wide blue arcs would dive under
the eves. He'd sit out through the poverty of the evening
and listen to voices overflow from the amusement park,
like the smell of cotton candy. Hungry,
he'd wander over to the refreshment stand,
order French fries and a Coke, only to discover
that the word for starlight had vanished
as had other words consigned to spontaneity's
leafy passages. All thoughts confined to memory,
which the more he'd try to access the more
it seemed he'd forgotten. Though there were times,
walking home, when he could almost remember

golden flowers in the wallpaper,
nights when his friends came over with a jug
of Carlo Rossi. And they'd talk almost until dawn,
the experience even as he was having it
gone, melted away, not an imprint preserved
in the daylight's famished vernacular.

John Clare in Santa Clara

He can't forget what this place used to be,
wind sending a flurry of apricot blossoms
falling from the one tree left in what once was an orchard.
Black-eyed Susans like helicopter blades in the ditches,
their wide eyes steering for the sun.

Home again, he's traded his Harley
for a Honda Civic. A casualty of the times, he knows
what one word can do to another. Storm clouds ride
over the mountains, the summits swathed in silver,
the slopes, rock-strewn and broken, clad with a glassy
    sheen.

The days are not long enough, the air glossy
with the sibilance of a desert oasis.
To calm himself he holds his breath, then lets it out,
his face a thicket knotted with the darkness
that stirs beneath the earth. Finally, the rain comes

that marks the ground he hopes not to die in
when the world shows signs of
sliding off its axis. He wants a life
that will not dissolve so quickly, clean
as terra-cotta, a protracted life of perpetual ease.

There is never enough sweetness in these
raindrops, as if they should be sugar
ricocheting off the pavement, not water
encrusting the cuffs of his trousers.
His mouth sharpened like a fox's or a badger's.

He's afraid he might swallow the flame of his tongue.
Then, they would certainly try to send him back
to where the locks are cinched at six o'clock,
and he behind a colony of doors would be
shut in, held fast, his red mind orbiting.

In a landscape hacked up and paved for tilt-ups,
he navigates from memory the blazing seam
of his garden—a good place to be buried. Although
he likes the airport, how dependably one can feel there
the tension of departure, the soul subject to inspection.

The only problem is that sometimes he can't
follow the arrows. And wanders the terminal,
knowing he's under suspicion, a traveler from home
moving dimly through the crowd, attempting
to get by, by not to standing out too far.

Coleridge in West Marin

Addicted to the alphabet, he stays up nights,
and mornings descends the path that winds past the lagoon
to the narrow wedge of beach, his breath blooming in the wind.
Unfinished pages on his desk, lines
eroding like the cliffs that crumble
more precipitously with each downpour
into the rock-ribbed sea crowding
the headland north of Bolinas.

His cottage on the mesa leaks, the pot-bellied stove
puts out more smoke than heat. Books heaped
on the floor, about to topple drunkenly as haystacks.
At his age he wonders what he writes for.
Crows roost in the eucalyptus across
the road—feathers iridescent
as the lining of a suit. He's quit
the San Francisco scene for good.

His wife and kids moved to West L.A. He visits
them occasionally, unable to endure the curdled air
or the miles of elevated concrete. He prefers
a less encumbered location, inventing
another self in the company of
younger women. Or observing an egret
in the eelgrass, impossibly balanced,
dredging his head though the water.

Tall bird, he preys on
whatever there is—small crabs, fingerlings,
anything he can slide down the hose of neck.

A bird doesn't want to know how good feeling bad can be,
nurturing his hunger, with the world in such abundance.
What reason is there to be depressed? Christ,
was anyone depressed before the nineteenth century,
or whined so damn much in verse about it?

He's begun to think of poetry as a form
of self-medication, a sort of substitute for love.
Or is it a kind of self-advertising? On the way home
he'll stop at Smiley's for a drink before
he enters the drizzle of afternoon. He thinks maybe
he should spend more time out, drive to Marshall to hear the new
Dead offshoot, or start that idyll on the new sewage plant—
or oh bloody hell, just screw it.

Close

While everyone else has gone to dinner
at the new Kurdish restaurant,
I sit here waiting for you.
I don't know why, as the day shrinks
to a close, we don't seem to get any closer.

As they say when one door closes,
another opens. I keep looking out the window
expecting your shadow to slip over the ivy.

But there was nothing except the paint mixer
of dusk, shaking out of itself
a facsimile of blackness. I knew then
that was the exact moment when
one particular something in my life was over.

I could recognize the mouth feel,
a taste of steel when my lips were closed,
and a numbness, as if all evening
I had been licking salt. The only thing
to do was to go to the convenience store.
and buy two pints of Häagen-Dazs.

Why do they put locks on doors of stores
that never close? I didn't see anyone in
the aisle dressed to purchase even an ounce
of beluga caviar. In fact, one ragged individual
screamed something that meant roughly
what was wrong with me. I don't know why

I am addicted to peeling insects
off my clothes and crushing their chitonous
shells. I am a connoisseur of the sound
of night pivoting on its hinges, sounds of
distant sirens and a helicopter
hovering over disheveled apartment blocks.

This is what happens when I spend a lot
of time alone: I find myself in a certain
brightly lit parking lot, in front of
the lurid entrance to an Indian
casino where I can almost taste my
luck run out. I was this close to losing
everything. I know I should have been shopping
for a healthy cereal, so many kinds of Kashi
now at Target down at the other end
of the mall. I know if I persevere
something good will come—it's happened before.

Look at me. Do I look like a person
who would wander around a discount store,
stuffing merchandise inside his coat? 'Course
not. I have a degree from a fine college,
live in a remodeled house. But where will I
find love? I drift wherever my thoughts take me.
Once a woman said I had a lovely speaking voice.

That I sounded exactly like William
Hurt. That I should make a tape of myself
reading Etruscan poetry, and send it to
the public radio station. That I
could help them raise money. And I almost
got on the air. That's as close as I've come

to the fame that I as an American feel
entitled to want. That's it—she never
called back. And right, as they say … no cigar.

Occupation

Something's wrong with the air, something yellow
that hides what's in plain sight. Streets caked with light
that sinks through layers of soot. The sun-choked
ground oozes a radiance. A smell so
nasty, you can only describe it in
the shards of your native language.
What a blast, everyday to go to work,
not knowing how or when you'll get it.

Introduced to the wire of smoke that will
be your ghost, the millennial trigger that
melts the gates of paradise. Any second
you can kiss your ass good-bye. Try to stay
cool, you understand you made a choice.
God and country. You signed up for
the drone of a cement mixer backing up
into a steel-walled driveway. A green
zone without trees, where there's a Burger King
around the corner across from the gym.

You can hook up a DVD, watch the big screen
like a trip to the spa. Or email
your photo home. You crave to be air-
conditioned. Better than trying to translate
the dialect of the wind. What do you call
sand shifting on a narrowing road,
or a ravine of Styrofoam? Give us
at least the shelter of a desktop
from these ten thousand pencils all trying
to affix one official signature.

This is how you wait to draw the short straw,
this is where your handprints are embedded.
Give us each day our daily lead. And lead
us not into perdition, a fusillade
of copper more deadly than an ex-wife's
phone call. Death is a summer movie,
a thrill for eighteen to twenty-four year olds

who sit and munch their popcorn in the dark,
worried if they'll ever get with someone
or be left to walk home smoldering
like saltpeter under the stars, no hook up
in the days ahead working at the car wash,
some glum unknown thing stirring in their veins.

What is Not Allowed

Lightning writes its name on the horizon
but no rain falls. It's an ill wind you've learned
that blows nobody good. Of course
you know it's not the wind that's ailing.

Beneath the veins of neon that thread the dark,
the town plaza is awash in the fumes of coffee grounds
and gasoline. Festooned with fangs of graffiti,
there's a sign that lists what is prohibited—

skateboarding, break dancing, gathering in groups
of more than four, despoiling
the plate glass kiosks that pop up
amid the bleak geometry like fungi.

An effervescent saxophone haze
wafts from the doorway of a Starbucks,
spreading its caffeinated narcolepsy among the patrons,
each staring meaningfully into their insulated cups,

picking at a dirty fingernail or scratching
their stubble as if sitting at a Parisian sidewalk café.
But here they are not allowed to smoke
or bring their dogs in with them

to sit across the table like a lover.
Here one is not allowed to read
over the shoulder another's newspaper
or to converse in Latin with the proprietor

of a flower shop. Here one is not allowed
to mention the crimes of weather or to shed
one's top to reveal a recent intimate tattoo.
Clothes must be the marquee,

the midriff-baring camisole top, the boxers
peeking out from under the waistband
of baggy low-slung jeans. One is not allowed
to shout the price of gold into a cell phone in Farsi

or in full view of the barista to sign
one's divorce decree. One is definitely not allowed
to blast hip-hop on a boom box, even on the corner,
or to ask the customers if they can spare any change.

No one is allowed to pay for drinks with pennies
pulled from a woolen sock.
Nor can one sit at a table without buying something.
The management will summon someone to move you along,

saying he has a bone to pick with you,
that he will adjust for you painlessly
if you cooperate. Otherwise he'll take you down
to the crossroads where you'll be lucky

if you keep any of your joints intact.
Evidently there's a convention of plainclothes men
up the street. Anything that you say
will surely be used against you. And anything

you wish to protest without the expressed
written consent of the police commissioner's office
and the mayor's reelection committee
is strictly prohibited.

Millennium Jukebox

Think we live in dangerous times.
Consider the 1640s.... Tell me
when a millennium wasn't mostly a catastrophe.
Falling towers, yes, and tribes of dark birds
slowly circling. *Repent Now* stenciled on breastplates,
graffitied on orphanages and stone bridges.

Fear number one on the charts,
playing in every roadhouse. You can't
turn down the volume because you don't like
the music. Every Roundhead on the dance floor
pushing and shoving. So go on, take
your sacraments; last rites are guaranteed.

Or you could try another epoch, say,
1790 or 1970. Although your neck might get caught under
the blade or splintered by twisted metal. The smell of burnt biosphere
on the breeze. You traded your chance to live
in Nice or San Francisco for a flat in Grozny
or Belfast or Zagreb, somewhere

night lays siege to the boulevards
and a yellow fog hunches against the window panes.
Snow scudding over Moscow apartment blocks,
rain battering Chicago Southside tenements.
Sand scouring the streets of East Jerusalem.
Manila filled with debris. Jakarta tangled in lightning.

The rain that floods Tennessee
sends a man into his burgundy Oldsmobile,

pushes him straight through to California,
a hundred miles an hour across the Bay Bridge,
pursued by the Highway Patrol, tires flattened by a SWAT team,
driving finally on his rims. Highway 101 closed.

So he douses himself with gasoline and,
after a four-and-a-half-hour standoff, is shot
with pressurized foam. He said he had
important things to do. Suppose you
had wandered out one evening,
gnats hovering above the embassies of grass,

the dusk the color of car sickness,
the air smelling faintly wounded,
and decided you too had had it. What music
would you bestow upon the customers of the corner café
you entered wearing your black skull cap
and your sash of bullets?

Or would you carry a corsage of fuses
onto the bus, counting backwards to yourself, ears plugged
into your iPod, and watch the dust
drifting through the fiery sunlight
as you grasp the sides of your seat, a prayer book
stuffed like a ticket in your back pocket?

Bombed

It looks as if a bomb's gone off behind the hills,
a smudge of smoke spreading beyond the unfinished
edge of dusk, the yellowed grass hunkered down against
the flaky dried-out clay our missions are made from.

Remember when it was duck and cover,
moving to the sound of the hydrogen jukebox,
marching in single file to a shelter in some school basement
stocked with phosphorescent peanuts,
a kind of canned meat, and the smell of ballast?

You remember when you ran through the woods, chased
by Weimaraners you surmised would go for the throat
protecting the big house whose owner crouched with
shotguns, keeping what was theirs. The ones who had
an Edsel in the driveway, a shiny new black
El Dorado in the garage, with a full tank.

A day didn't go by you didn't think about annihilation,
the way it happened in movies, a *Twilight Zone*
where the last two people on earth couldn't love each other
although it meant the end of the species, sulking
in separate corners, hoarding their cans of Vienna
sausage, calculating how long they can hold out.

Those movies bombed when they came out, like "Little Boy"
re-released in the creases of the mind, as dust
and ashes settle, make monochromatic the afternoons
that this time of year should blaze overhead, such flaming
sunsets ... like the beings we've imagined seeing, bombed
out of our minds, who live peacefully on other planets.

Recovery at Lake Tahoe

The rocky beach shines in mid-August
late afternoon sun between shadows
of Ponderosa pines. Ripples stripe the water
near shore. Across the lake blue deepens
into troughs of indigo. Far out, I imagine,
the wind swells. But here it is benign,
the leaves of manzanita, at the
periphery already beginning to yellow,
barely move. A brownish blackbird,
probably female, chirrups beneath a thicket
of deerbrush, while a Chris-Craft throttles
back its engines approaching the pier,
reggae blaring. The young man driving
and his passenger shed their sky blue T-shirts
as they pass, letting another kid jump on
before roaring out again, spraying up
a frothy wake. I try to stay in the present,
disengaged from what seems to move too fast.
Around me the world strives to maintain
a good mood. Two girls in red swimsuits,
approaching adolescence, half-immersed, agitate
in the mottled water. Everything seems
to be calling out, *too soon, too soon.*
A blackbird flashes its yellow eyes
as it plunges its wing feathers into the
glassy curl at the shoreline's edge.
Euphagus cyanocephalus.
The end of summer presses down
through the alders with an urgent sweetness.
We do what we can to deny what Keats

with some reluctance was forced to accept—
the exhaustion of the inexhaustible. So I
must learn to look more closely, to count
the number of pine needles in a cluster,
to know things by their proper names. To smell
wood smoke hovering over a metal
picnic table set with a checkered cloth.
Five little girls in bright towels and hoodies
scuffing rocks. While a blackbird fluffs
its feathers on a lakefront post beside
an empty table, standing on one foot.

Goofy Foot

While I'm doing something else—writing
checks, adding up my deductions—you remind me
I better get cracking on poetry. You caution
me not to get obsessed with the Olympics,
watching to see who's favored
for the gold medal in the apocalypse.

I notice you put your right foot forward
when you stand up on your board.
It's me who's the one that's wrong-footed,
trying to be regular, trying to remember
to clean the counter. If there's something I could do
I'd be neater. Even a seal could keep house better.

I don't know why I am the way I am.
Even getting an eyelash in my eye
is reason enough for me to run off the rails.
Is that obsession or helplessness?
You go out every morning dressed to the nines,
while for me the variants of clothing are inexplicable.

You think more about your clothes
than the meaning that's been removed
from your alimentary canal, the part put in a jar,
you didn't need, pungent with information.
In the cartoon the dim-witted coyote doesn't know
he's gone off a cliff, legs churning in blue air.

Until it's too late. Every morning
I face the mirror and try to scrape the worries

off my face. And always you rebound
into the perfect hemoglobin of the day,
grateful you live in a place where wild mustard
flowers in February amidst the fusty backyards.

I don't want to discuss what happens after
the plum tree drops its blossoms, after the green
starts to fray from the grass. For now
I'm content to let the clock spin forward,
to watch the athletes surf down the slushy hill,
crouched, zigzagging around gates.

Each inside her helmet, balancing on an edge,
carving a thin groove in the snow, tilting
her body as if by instinct or faith the way she wants
to go, leaning not to fall in the icy murk,
skimming the slope with a forearm, locked in,
earbuds plugged into her ears, soaked in her own music.

Twirl

They're always in the back, the ones who spin
around. Fair-haired, dreadlocked, the skinny one
whose hands flutter as if controlled by wires.
Here's one in a red bandana dress, face
clenched, who bats invisible moths that
tickle her fingers. There's another who
whirls as if the fine hairs glistening on
her mini-skirted legs had just caught fire.
The lead guitarist stranded on the desert
island of the stage throws back his head
as if conjuring birdcalls, plays a riff
that flies into the tropical heat, and turns
the crowd into a pack of howling dogs
trying to catch the scent of paradise,
while the organist grinds his radioactive
chords, a whine that glitters in the mix.
The one in a black headband, bare midriff,
suddenly rising to her feet, her hands
swimming above her shoulders, transcendent
as an evangelist's, waving now like
someone needing to be saved, who won't be
rescued. The tide taking her further and
further out. Her partner, a grizzled blond
maybe once a surfer, pistons his arms,
a Cardinal sweatshirt tied like a bag
of blood around his waist, makes no progress
towards her. His fists, self-absorbed, tearing out
chunks of air while the other dancers step
around him, pogo-ing their necks to see
the unseen thing that forces them forward,

or what keeps them spinning further into
the alcoves of their hair, into ghostlier
recesses of the room where a woman
draped in a gauze of scarves can twirl until
no self is left, only a mineral
silhouette, a semblance of flesh whirled
in the centrifuge of the music, 'round
and 'round until she becomes something else.

Novel

I wait at the vet for news of my cat,
whether they'll need to take X-rays or not.
I sit on a green plastic cushion and listen
to his cries as they squeeze to feel
his insides. A young assistant comes
out, wearing a smock like pajamas,
sleepy-eyed, brushing her hair's weight off her face,
says they need to take one picture and draw blood.
I can still hear him in the back, and can imagine
how scared he is because I am that way
about everything that hurts.

Then the Dutch door swings open and out
flounces an Airedale in a teal bandana.
The owner flouncing too, almost
giggling, tugs on the leash and shouts
"come Steinbeck" at the beast, looking at no one
in particular. It's the first time I've heard
that name given to an animal. Happiness
wags its tail beside her. A new dog
comes in—a Samoyed nervous as the blade
of a windmill. He's called Clyde—a good name—
his blue-jeaned, T-shirted owner leads him
through the waiting room, where he stops at the desk
to chat with the just-out-of-school receptionist.

My head's filled up, a low-grade fever,
I sweat just enough to be uncomfortable
my skin slick as the waxed coat of an apple.
How not delicious this is to await the outcome,

feeling the body's heat and darkness. Why would I
speak to the new woman who's come in,
overly made-up in the tight sleeveless burgundy sweater,
whose chest juts out? Literature is preparation for a life
never to be lived, so the critic says. So why do I wonder
what her life is like with the two Chihuahuas
they bring her, yapping like a pair of thorns
that dig into the silence, my privacy plundered.
O, I'll never know what cuts her heart.

She says nothing as she walks past,
looking at the empty crate beside me,
about what it feels like to be inside her body.
And I don't want to know. I can't even
imagine. All this to distract time, to keep
me from thinking the worst things.
The leukemia that lurks inside the city's
bloodstream. The heart clogged with worms
beginning to stretch their elongated mouths.
I hear the call of the nocturnal, the plaintive
whine of electricity feeding the clock.

How I am going to sit here looking up
at the basket of miniature Hershey bars
wrapped in Easter colors before I begin
to lose it, to pace up and down, my tongue
lolling out. To start panting and
fill my pockets. I get up to read
the flea management brochures, the fluorescents
vibrating the way they do, my eyes suddenly stuttering.
This is something new. The hero wants
to pause the story and have a snack.

There's a clamor in the antechamber,
a slinky Labrador nearly scales
the counter. She's got the leash in her mouth.
Finally my gray twenty-pounder comes out,
collapsed into himself like an overwatered plant.
They've injected saline solution into his back,
it's made a hump, and I'm warned his legs and paws
could swell up, not to be alarmed. He won't eat
or drink I say. Perhaps he has a sore throat,
perhaps his stomach hurts. It's been
three days and we're no better
than the sky perforated with pollen and
a skeleton of rain. It could be allergies
or an infection. Who knows. Both of us are
miserable, riding the wheel of misfortune.
Is this new? Who will love us
if we ask the world for it?

Notes

"Beyond Where I Ever Traveled"
Reference to e.e. cummings, "somewhere i have never travelled, gladly beyond." The beach mentioned is Mission Beach in San Diego.

"Sense of Place"
President Theodore Roosevelt joined John Muir on a three-day camping trip in Yosemite, during which time Muir persuaded President Roosevelt to protect Yosemite Valley and the Mariposa Grove of giant sequoias as part of Yosemite National Park. The lines "A man who does not live in nature / as a stone does or an animal, / will never in his life / write two worthwhile lines" are quoted from Issak Babel's story "Awakening," translated by David McDuff (Penguin edition).

"Palm Haven"
The Palm Haven development of craftsman-style homes dates from 1913, and is situated just southwest of downtown San Jose.

"The Beginning of Summer"
Lines from John Clare's (1793–1864) poem "First Love," thought to have been written in 1841.

"Fall"
Lines from Victoria Chang's poem "October," published in *Salvinia Molesta* (University of Georgia Press, 2008). Larry Levis (1946–96), poet born in Fresno, California.

"Melville"
Reference to Herman Melville (1819–91); also to Melvyl, the catalog of the University of California Libraries.

"Country"
Wayne's World (1992), a film starring Dana Carvey and Mike Myers, set in Aurora, Illinois.

"In the Buddha Factory"
The Tiantai Buddha carvings factory, near Taintai City in Zhejiang Province, China.

"Wandering Around"
"Walking Around" by Pablo Neruda (1904–73).

"El Eden"
An eco-park on the former set of *Predator* (1987) starring Arnold Schwarzenegger, south of Puerto Vallarta, Mexico. Also reference to *The Night of the Iguana* (1964), a film written by Tennessee Williams, directed by John Huston, and starring Richard Burton, Eva Gardner, and Deborah Kerr, filmed near the small village of Mismaloya, on the coast of the Bahia de Banderas, Jalisco, Mexico.

"Slight"
Adapts lines from William Blake's (1757–1827) poem "Garden of Love."

"Hyperreal: Virgil in Los Angeles"
Sandow Birk's three paintings based on Dante's *The Divine Comedy*, in the collection of the San Jose Museum of Art. Variation on Wallace Stevens' poem "The Pleasures of Merely Circulating" (1934).

"Sympathy for the Devil"
Charles Simic's poem "Brooms."

"Of Its Occasion"
Title refers to Wallace Stevens' "An Ordinary Evening in New Haven," pt. XII. Includes references to "Domination of Black" and "Bantams in Pine Woods."

"Wordsworth in Santa Cruz"
Love Creek Road in the rural mountain area north of Santa Cruz is prone to destructive landslides. Pedestrian mall in downtown Santa Cruz, severely damaged by the 1989 Loma Prieta earthquake. Steamer Lane, a famous surfing location located in a residential area near downtown Santa Cruz.

"John Clare in Santa Clara"
Two of John Clare's best-known nature poems are "The Fox" and "The Badger."

"Bombed"
"Little Boy" was the code name for the atomic bomb dropped on Hiroshima, Japan, on August 6, 1945.

"Goofy Foot"
A phrase in snowboarding or surfboarding meaning a riding stance in which one leads with the right foot.

About the Author

Alan Soldofsky has published three chapbooks of poems: *Kenora Station*, *Staying Home*, and *Holding Adam/My Father's Books* (which includes a selection of poems by his son, Adam Soldofsky). He was the recipient of a 2009 Artist Fellowship in Literary Arts from Arts Council Silicon Valley. His poems and criticism have appeared in *The Gettysburg Review*, *The Georgia Review*, *The Greensboro Review*, *The Nation*, *The North American Review*, *Poetry Flash*, *Poetry East West*, *Rattle*, *The Rattling Wall*, and *The Writer's Chronicle*, among other publications. He directs the Creative Writing Program at San Jose State University where he is a professor of English and comparative literature. He also has taught at the University of California, Berkeley, and the University of San Francisco. He has been a contributing editor of *Poetry Flash* (the literary review and calendar for the West), a producer/host of literary programs at KPFA-FM, Berkeley, and editorial director of the Commonwealth Club of California weekly newsletter, serving under club president Amb. Shirley Temple Black. He grew up in Iowa City and received an MFA from the University of Iowa Writers' Workshop.